# Vegetarianism and Teens

Cult Awareness
**A Hot Issue**
ISBN 0-7660-1196-8

Cyberdanger and
Internet Safety
**A Hot Issue**
ISBN 0-7660-1368-5

Date Rape
**A Hot Issue**
ISBN 0-7660-1198-4

Drug Abuse
and Teens
**A Hot Issue**
ISBN 0-7660-1372-3

Eating Disorders
**A Hot Issue**
ISBN 0-7660-1336-7

Endangered Animals
of North America
**A Hot Issue**
ISBN 0-7660-1373-1

Hate and Racist
Groups
**A Hot Issue**
ISBN 0-7660-1371-5

Multiethnic Teens
and Cultural Identity
**A Hot Issue**
ISBN 0-7660-1201-8

Runaway Teens
**A Hot Issue**
ISBN 0-7660-1640-4

Sexually Transmitted
Diseases
**A Hot Issue**
ISBN 0-7660-1192-5

Stalking
**A Hot Issue**
ISBN 0-7660-1364-2

Teens,
Depression,
and the Blues
**A Hot Issue**
ISBN 0-7660-1369-3

Teens and
Pregnancy
**A Hot Issue**
ISBN 0-7660-1365-0

Teen Privacy
Rights
**A Hot Issue**
ISBN 0-7660-1374-X

Teen Smoking and
Tobacco Use
**A Hot Issue**
ISBN 0-7660-1359-6

The Women's
Movement
and Young Women
Today
**A Hot Issue**
ISBN 0-7660-1200-X

# Vegetarianism and Teens

## A Hot Issue

### Kathleen Winkler

**Enslow Publishers, Inc.**

40 Industrial Road          PO Box 38
Box 398                     Aldershot
Berkeley Heights, NJ 07922  Hants GU12 6BP
USA                         UK

http://www.enslow.com

**Library of Congress Cataloging-in-Publication Data**

Winkler, Kathleen.
Vegetarianism and teens : a hot issue / Kathleen Winkler.
        p.  cm.—(Hot issues)
Includes bibliographical references and index.
ISBN 0-7660-1375-8
1. Vegetarianism—Juvenile literature. [1. Vegetarianism.]
I. Title. II. Series.
RM236 .W55   2000
613.2'62—dc21

                                        00-010951

Printed in the United States of America

10 9 8 7 6 5 4 3 2 1

**To Our Readers:**
All Internet Addresses in this book were active and appropriate when we
went to press. Any comments or suggestions can be sent by e-mail to
Comments@enslow.com or to the address on the back cover.

**Illustration Credits:** Corel Corporation, pp. 3 (background), 8, 9,
11, 16 (t.l., t.r., b.r.), 21, 23, 25, 28, 31, 33, 35, 51; Courtesy of the
United Soybean Board, p. 16 (b.l.); Enslow Publishers, Inc., pp. 3
(foreground), 47; LifeART 1998 Lippincott Williams & Wilkins,
p. 42; Robert Sebree/PETA, p. 18.

**Cover Illustration:** Corel Corporation (background) and Enslow
Publishers, Inc. (foreground)

# Contents

# Chapter 1

# Meet Some Vegetarians

Lynn has never eaten fish. She has not eaten chicken since she was in eighth grade. She has not eaten beef since she was a sophomore in high school. "The last piece of pepperoni pizza I popped into my mouth was during my junior year in high school," she says.[1] Lynn did not decide to give up eating meat all at once. Instead, it was a gradual process.

"It came at different ages for different things," she says. "I never liked fish or seafood from the time I was a little girl. I didn't like the smell, I didn't like the taste, so I never ate them. But I did eat chicken, turkey, hamburgers, hot dogs."[2]

## Giving Up Meat

When Lynn was in eighth grade, she stopped eating poultry. Then, in tenth grade science class, Lynn studied food safety and learned about the dirty conditions in some meat-packing plants. She remembered her fifth grade science class when they studied tapeworms and the reasons to cook meat until it is well done. "That pretty much ended my meat eating," she laughs.[3]

Lynn's mother was not happy. "She thought I was going to die of malnutrition, meat-and-potatoes lady that she is," Lynn remembers. "Every time I got sick, she'd blame it on my not eating meat."[4]

Finally, Lynn agreed to go to a registered dietitian. A dietitian is someone who has studied human nutrition and helps people plan what they eat. The dietitian asked Lynn to write down everything she ate for two weeks. Then Lynn took a blood test to see if she was low in any vitamins or iron. Based on all that information, the dietitian told Lynn that she was getting enough protein in her vegetarian diet, but she was a little low in the minerals iron and

*V*egetables and fruits are a major part of a vegetarian diet. Foods such as grains, nuts, and other sources of nutrients are also very important.

*V*egetarians can often create full meals from side dishes when meat is being served. Sometimes, however, this can result in an unbalanced meal.

calcium. The dietitian recommended that Lynn take some supplements (vitamins and minerals in pill form) to make sure she was getting enough of these two minerals.

Lynn's mother did not change her cooking for Lynn, so her dad and two sisters did not get upset. In fact, they really did not notice. "I'd eat the vegetables, side dishes like rice or potatoes and a salad," she says. "No one complained. I think my dad thought I'd grow out of it if no one made a big deal about it."[5]

Most of Lynn's high school friends did not know what she was doing. "I wasn't eating anything weird. I'd just bring a peanut butter and jelly or cheese sandwich—not that much different from what they were eating," she says. "A few of them would say, 'but you wear leather shoes', and I'd explain that it was because of taste that I didn't eat meat."[6]

The only problem came when she went to

friends' houses for dinner, or to a school party where the only food was hot dogs. She would fill up on rolls, cheese, and dessert. That made for some unbalanced meals, but it did not happen often.

# Living Away From Home

Things got easier during Lynn's first two years of college, when she lived in a dorm. The cafeteria had a salad bar, and there was always pasta or some other side dish she could eat.

During her last two years of college, Lynn moved into an apartment. It was during this time that her diet was at its worst. She did not like to cook, so she would not think about food until she was so hungry she needed to eat *right now*. Too often a glass of milk, a bag of microwave popcorn, or a bowl of ice cream was dinner. "I was very lucky that the way I was eating didn't harm my health," she says. "I was tired a lot, but then most college students getting by on five or six hours of sleep are tired."[7]

Things changed again when she met Brad, the young man she would marry after college. "He noticed what I was eating—and he was upset!" she says. "He moved his cookware into my apartment and started making dinner for us a couple of times a week."[8]

Brad and Lynn, now both in their early thirties, have learned a lot about eating a nutritious vegetarian diet. Brad did not become a vegetarian but he eats many meatless meals. They were willing to do the learning and planning that all vegetarians must do to stay healthy.

Lynn also points out that being a vegetarian has become easier in the last few years. There are many vegetarian cookbooks available, and most grocery stores now have a vegetarian section. In addition to fresh foods and other selections, there are often several meatless frozen dinners and brands of tofu or frozen vegetarian burgers to choose from. Restaurants, too, have more vegetarian choices. Even fast food chains now have baked potatoes or vegetarian burgers and tacos. Lynn keeps frozen veggie burgers in the freezer so when she and Brad go to a cookout they can take a couple along. "If you saw me eating one, you'd never know it was a veggie burger. It just looks like I'm eating a hamburger along with everyone else!" she says.[9]

## Other Experiences

Lynn is certainly not the only teenager who has turned vegetarian—they are everywhere. Kristie was just fifteen when she won a writing contest with her essay on why she became a vegetarian. Her original reason, she wrote, was that she wanted to lose weight and get in better shape. By eating bagels for breakfast, fruit for lunch, and vegetables with a

veggie burger or bean soup for dinner, she has improved the way she feels and looks, she wrote in her essay. It was published in a magazine for vegetarians.[10]

Brad, Lynn's husband, eats many vegetarian meals with her. But, being a naturally thin person, he found it was hard to keep enough weight on his frame when he was not eating any meat. "I got too thin at one point," he says. "Now I eat some meat and use a protein drink when I need it to keep my weight up. But I still enjoy many vegetarian dishes."[11]

Not all teens have the good experience that Lynn and Kristie did from taking meat out of their diets. For example, Debbie Siefert, a teenager from Illinois, says she has had an eating disorder since she was a child. She would either eat too much or starve herself. At one point she decided to become a vegetarian. She says she did it both to rebel against her parents (her father was a butcher) and to avoid the fat and calories in meat. She is now in treatment for her eating disorder. Although still a vegetarian, Debbie says she is now adding more foods to her diet and taking in more calories to maintain a healthy weight.[12]

Being a vegetarian has become a popular thing to do among teenagers. It can be a healthy way to eat. But, without learning and planning, it can also lead to problems. Some vegetarian teens do not plan their diets carefully. They put their health at risk by not getting enough vitamins and minerals.

# Chapter 2

# Who Is a Vegetarian?

Every day thousands of teens sit down to lunch with their friends in their school cafeterias. Because they are in a hurry to finish their lunches in time for biology class, or are listening to the latest gossip about who is going to the big dance, they may not even notice what their friends are eating. The first choice for lunch for most of them is probably a hamburger or a hot dog. But chances are good that a couple of people around the table are not eating either one. Instead, they might be munching a vegetable burrito, a plate of stir-fried vegetables and rice, or a salad, if the cafeteria offers them. Students who bring lunch from home may be eating a peanut butter and jelly or egg-salad sandwich with a side of carrot sticks.

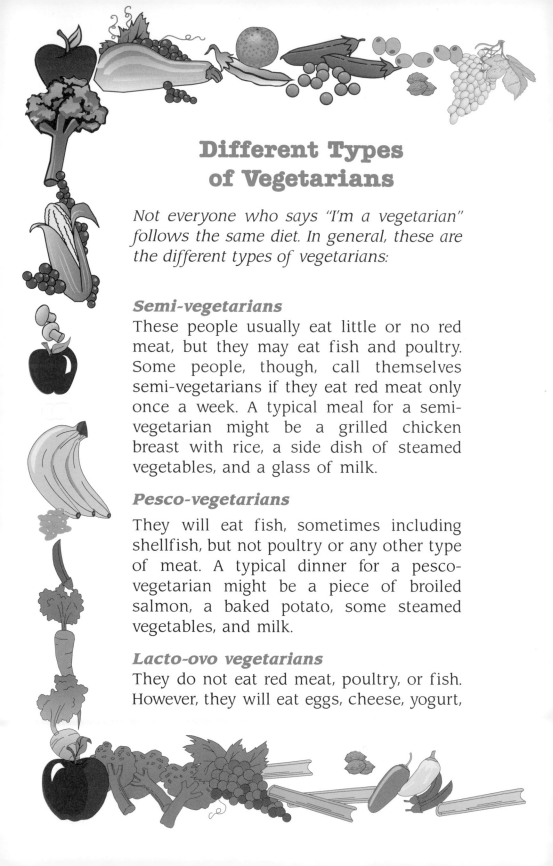

# Different Types of Vegetarians

*Not everyone who says "I'm a vegetarian" follows the same diet. In general, these are the different types of vegetarians:*

### Semi-vegetarians

These people usually eat little or no red meat, but they may eat fish and poultry. Some people, though, call themselves semi-vegetarians if they eat red meat only once a week. A typical meal for a semi-vegetarian might be a grilled chicken breast with rice, a side dish of steamed vegetables, and a glass of milk.

### Pesco-vegetarians

They will eat fish, sometimes including shellfish, but not poultry or any other type of meat. A typical dinner for a pesco-vegetarian might be a piece of broiled salmon, a baked potato, some steamed vegetables, and milk.

### Lacto-ovo vegetarians

They do not eat red meat, poultry, or fish. However, they will eat eggs, cheese, yogurt,

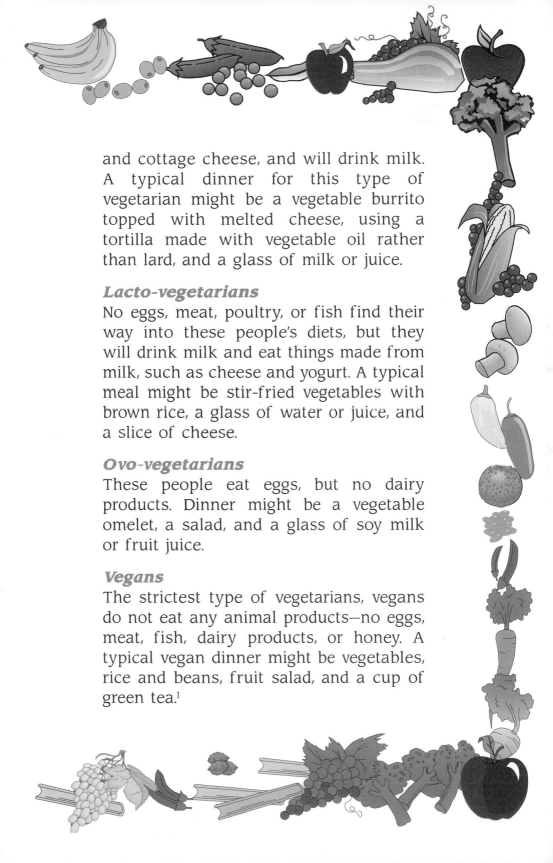

and cottage cheese, and will drink milk. A typical dinner for this type of vegetarian might be a vegetable burrito topped with melted cheese, using a tortilla made with vegetable oil rather than lard, and a glass of milk or juice.

### Lacto-vegetarians

No eggs, meat, poultry, or fish find their way into these people's diets, but they will drink milk and eat things made from milk, such as cheese and yogurt. A typical meal might be stir-fried vegetables with brown rice, a glass of water or juice, and a slice of cheese.

### Ovo-vegetarians

These people eat eggs, but no dairy products. Dinner might be a vegetable omelet, a salad, and a glass of soy milk or fruit juice.

### Vegans

The strictest type of vegetarians, vegans do not eat any animal products—no eggs, meat, fish, dairy products, or honey. A typical vegan dinner might be vegetables, rice and beans, fruit salad, and a cup of green tea.[1]

*A* semi-vegetarian meal might include chicken or even, occasionally, red meat. Pesco-vegetarians eat fish, but not poultry or other meat. Quiche can be a good dish for lacto-ovo vegetarians, since it is made with eggs and dairy products. The vegan meal at the bottom left includes no animal products.

# A Growing Number of Vegetarians

Some people may just have an occasional meatless meal, but others have chosen to remove meat from their diets altogether. More and more teens are becoming vegetarians. Some of them talk about it whenever they can and try to get their friends to join them. Others change their diets quietly. Their friends may not even notice.

About five million Americans over the age of 18, or 2.5 percent of the adult population, were vegetarians according to a national Zogby Poll sponsored by the Vegetarian Resource Group in 2000. (Zogby considered people who never ate meat, poultry, or fish to be vegetarians.) About twice as many women as men fit into this category. Vegetarianism was also more common among younger people, with 6 percent of people from ages 18 to 29 considered vegetarians. In a Zogby poll of teenagers from ages 13 to 17, 11 percent of girls and 5 percent of boys were counted as vegetarians.[2]

# What Is a Vegetarian?

Most vegetarians do not eat meat, poultry, fish, or, in some cases, eggs and dairy products. (Vegetarians who eliminate all animal products from their diet are called vegans.) Instead, they eat a diet rich in vegetables, fruit, grains, nuts, and seeds. People follow a vegetarian diet for many different reasons. Some people do not eat meat because of ethical or religious concerns. Some eat a meatless diet because they are concerned about their health.[3] However, many vegetarians simply prefer fresh, unprocessed foods and do not care to eat meat.

**LIVE AND LET LIVE!**
**GO VEGETARIAN**

Jennie Garth
and Frida

**PETA** PEOPLE FOR THE ETHICAL TREATMENT OF ANIMALS
P.O. BOX 42516, WASHINGTON, DC 20015 • 301-770-PETA

*M*any celebrities have become vegetarians because of their concern for animal rights. Some, like Jennie Garth, have supported organizations such as People for the Ethical Treatment of Animals (PETA).

Teens who are interested in becoming vegetarians might like to know about some famous people who are vegetarians. Celebrities Paul McCartney, Michael J. Fox, k.d. lang, Lenny Kravitz, Brad Pitt, Drew Barrymore, and Jennie Garth are some well-known vegetarians. There are many others.[4]

But vegetarianism is not a new phenomenon. Greek philosophers Epicurus (342–270 B.C.) and Plutarch (46–120 A.D.) were both vegetarians. Scientists Sir Isaac Newton (1642–1727), Charles Darwin (1809–1882), Thomas Edison (1847–1931), and Albert Einstein (1879–1955) were vegetarians as well. Clara Barton (1821–1912), humanitarian and founder of the American Red Cross, and Susan B. Anthony (1820–1906), one of the first leaders of the campaign for women's right to vote, were also both vegetarians.[5]

Teens looking into vegetarianism also might find it interesting to learn about people from other cultures and their diets. While many Americans, especially teens, build a diet around fast-food hamburgers and steaks, people in many other cultures base their diets on vegetables and grains. People from India, China, Japan, and Mexico eat more grains and less meat than most Americans do.

That does not mean that all people in those countries are vegetarians. Instead, most of them eat only a little meat, using it as a side dish or to add flavor to other dishes. Their main dish usually is made from grains and vegetables. Teens can learn more about how people in those cultures eat by reading Indian, Chinese, Japanese, or Mexican cookbooks, or going to restaurants that serve the foods of those countries.

# Chapter 3

# Why Become a Vegetarian?

**W**hy would a teen want to sing in the school chorus? Because he loves to sing? Because her friends are all in the chorus? There can be many reasons for doing something. It is the same with becoming a vegetarian. Not everyone does it for the same reason.

## History of Vegetarianism

Despite the popular view of our prehistoric ancestors being club-wielding hunters, early humans ate a diet consisting mostly of roots, berries, and whatever plant life they could gather. Their meat intake was limited because they lacked the tools and skills to successfully hunt animals. Over time, as people became better hunters and farmers, meat began to assume a larger part in the human diet.[1] Human beings are omnivorous, meaning they eat both animal and plant life. But still, in many cultures people eat very little meat.

Many people practice vegetarianism as part of

*V*egetarianism is a part of many world religions. Hindus and Buddhists have practiced vegetarianism for thousands of years. Pictured here are Buddhist monks at prayer.

their religion. Hindus and Buddhists have been following a vegetarian or semi-vegetarian diet for thousands of years. Within the Roman Catholic Church, Trappist monks have been vegetarian since 1666. In the nineteenth century, members of the Bible Christian sect established the first vegetarian groups in England and the United States.

However, the vegetarian diet did not become popular in the Western world until the 1960s. During that time, people were becoming more interested in following a healthier lifestyle. New studies were showing that eating a diet high in animal fat increased a person's risk of heart disease. Other research discovered the important role fiber plays in the human diet.

People were also learning about the inhumane and unhealthy ways some farm animals were being raised. As the population around the world had grown, small family-owned farms were no longer able to meet the demand for food. Large agricultural corporations began taking over smaller traditional farms. They were able to produce a much greater amount of food for less money.

Unfortunately, as these agribusinesses grew larger, a practice called "factory farming" began. In order to save money, some corporate owners took shortcuts with the health and well-being of the animals. Many farm animals were kept in pens or cages too small for their needs. They often became sick. Many people objected to eating meat for these reasons.

Over time, the meat, poultry, dairy, and egg industries began to use drugs, hormones, and other chemicals on the animals to keep them healthy and productive. Some people decided to stop eating

*M*any people become vegetarians because they care about animals. They do not like the idea of animals being killed for food. Others object to the way some farm animals are raised.

meat because of the medicines and chemicals being fed to farm animals. They were concerned that these chemicals might remain in the meat of the animals. Therefore, a person eating a hamburger might also consume the hormones or chemicals that were fed to the cattle.[2]

# Some Reasons Why Teens Become Vegetarians

Some people, like Lynn, just do not like the taste or texture of meat. Since they do not like it, and do not like the flavor meat gives to other foods cooked with it, they stop eating meat and usually will not eat foods like soup made with a meat stock.

Some teenagers care a lot about the environment. They have learned things that trouble them about how cattle are raised and meat is produced. For example, 45 percent of the land in the United States is used for grazing and growing grain to feed cattle, hogs, and other livestock. Forty percent of the world's grain supply is used to feed animals; in the United States it is nearly 70 percent. It takes seven pounds of grain to produce a pound of pork, five for a pound of beef, and three for a pound of chicken.[3] Some people think it would be more efficient to feed the grain directly to people instead of to animals.

Other reasons related to the environment include the fact that it takes a lot of water to produce meat. In the Western states as much as 70 percent of the water goes into meat production through watering the animals and growing their food. And pollution can be a by-product of meat production. For example, teens who have had a pet are probably familiar with the problem of dog waste lying around

*M*any forests have been cut down for pasture land. Some teens have become vegetarians because of such environmental concerns.

the yard. Think of what pastures full of cattle, pens full of hogs, and sheds full of chickens leave behind. Even though some is used to make fertilizer, animal waste washes into rivers and streams and is a big cause of water pollution.[4]

Grazing animals and growing food for them also harms the land. Topsoil can wash away and a green pasture can turn to desert when it has too many animals grazing on it. Rain forests in Central and South America have been cut down to make room for pasture land and to grow cattle food. Many of the plants and animals that once lived in these forests are now extinct, largely due to the loss of their habitat.

Some people become vegetarians because they care about animals. Researchers at TBWA-Chiat/Day, an advertising firm in Chicago, studied teens' reasons for becoming vegetarians. They found that animal rights was the number one reason.[5] Some teens just cannot bring themselves to eat anything that once walked around. Their love for their pets may extend to include all animals. They worry about the ways in which cattle and poultry are raised on farms and about how they are killed. Not eating meat, they feel, spares animals from dying.

Some teenagers worry about hormones and antibiotics that are fed to cattle and other livestock to keep them healthy. They are concerned about pesticides used to grow food for livestock. Teens also worry about bacteria growing in meat and other foods. They do not want any of that in the food they eat.

There is some basis for their concern. Traces of hormones, pesticides, and antibiotics have been found in meat. And people in several cities have gotten food poisoning from E. coli and salmonella bacteria in undercooked meat and other food. These bacteria can be spread by poor sanitation when preparing food.[6] In Milwaukee, Wisconsin, for example, more than 500 people became sick and one child died from eating the food served at two locations of a chain restaurant in the summer of 2000. It was later found that some employees had been washing their hands in a bucket of contaminated water. Others had been slicing watermelon on cutting boards that had been used for beef and not properly washed.[7]

Although following a fad is not a good reason to

choose a diet, some teenagers do see being a vegetarian as a way to be part of an "in" group. Many movie stars and musicians are vegetarians and appear at animal rights rallies. Teens may see many of their friends jumping aboard the vegetarian wagon, and a lot of teenagers like to do what their friends are doing. And some may see being a vegetarian as an easy way to be "different" from their parents.

Some people are vegetarians for religious reasons. Seventh-Day Adventists believe that to have a healthy body you should not drink alcohol or smoke; many also do not eat meat. Many people who follow Eastern religions such as Buddhism and Hinduism are vegetarians. Although the Jewish faith does not require its members to be vegetarians, a few do so because following a kosher diet, which does not allow mixing meat and dairy products, is made easier by eliminating meat.

Some people become vegetarians because they believe it is a healthier way to eat and control their weight. If they plan their vegetarian diet carefully, they may be right. Teens who are concerned about their weight should talk to their parents and a doctor, a school nurse, or a dietitian before making changes to their diet.

# The Health Benefits of Being a Vegetarian

"In the overall picture, a vegetarian diet can be healthier than the usual teen diet of [burgers] and fast-food fried chicken," says Rebekah Wang-Cheng, M.D., a doctor of internal medicine and associate professor of medicine at the Medical College of Wisconsin. She has been a vegetarian herself since she was a child. "There are some important things people going on a vegetarian diet need to know about, but by and large it is a healthy diet for teenagers and children."[8]

"There is a lot of evidence that people who follow a vegetarian diet have lower rates of disease in the arteries that bring blood to their hearts," says Joan Pleuss, a registered dietitian at the Medical College of Wisconsin who works in medical research. "They also have lower rates of high blood pressure and some types of cancer."[9] Although teenagers do not often get these illnesses, doctors say healthy living to prevent these problems starts during childhood and the teen years.

*Coronary artery disease.* Imagine the arteries, the vessels that carry blood around the body, as garden hoses. If a hose is clogged, water cannot get through. If arteries are blocked with a sticky fat called cholesterol, blood cannot get to the heart and the person may have a heart attack. A vegetarian diet is naturally low in saturated fat and cholesterol so arteries do not become clogged as easily. One study published in the *New England Journal of Medicine* showed

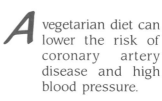

*A* vegetarian diet can lower the risk of coronary artery disease and high blood pressure.

that people who ate soy protein instead of animal protein lowered their cholesterol levels by as much as 10 percent.[10]

*High blood pressure.* The heart is a powerful pump that moves blood through the body's system of blood vessels. It takes a certain amount of pressure to keep the blood moving; otherwise it would just pool in one place. If the amount of force, called the blood pressure, is too high, it can harm the arteries or kidneys. It might also cause a heart attack or stroke (a burst blood vessel in the brain). A vegetarian diet can lower the risk of high blood pressure because less force is needed to move blood through arteries not clogged with fat.[11]

*Cancer.* Research into diet as a factor in cancer is a hot topic. Some doctors think that as much as two-thirds of adult cancers are related to diet. Doctors are finding that antioxidants in food help protect against the disease. Many antioxidants are found in fruits and vegetables, which are of course a big part of a vegetarian diet. In one study, Seventh Day Adventists who were vegetarians had lower rates of cancer and heart disease than those who ate meat.[12]

In addition, a vegetarian diet can help people control their weight. "Vegetarians tend to weigh less," says Joan Pleuss. "If you are following a vegetarian diet you eat a lot less fat. And you do eat a lot more vegetables and grains. They are all low-fat, low-calorie foods."[13]

It sounds like a vegetarian diet is nothing but good news. But that is not necessarily so. There can be serious problems if a vegetarian diet is not carefully planned.

# Chapter 4

# Precautions to Keep in Mind

**T**here are many good reasons for becoming a vegetarian. However, there are some things teens should know if they are going to start eating vegetarian. If they are uninformed, they can actually harm their bodies.

## Vegetarians Need Balanced Diets

"I don't recommend that children and teenagers go on vegetarian diets," says Dr. Craig Leach, D.O., a pediatrician who is chief of the pediatrics section at the Children's Hospital of Wisconsin in Milwaukee. "Vegetarianism isn't usually done in a careful way by children and teens. They often leave out important parts of good nutrition because of eating fast food or peer pressure and still think they are on a vegetarian diet. What they are really on is an unhealthy diet."[1]

He described what he might say to a teenager who has come to him for a checkup and plans to become a vegetarian. "I ask, 'What does that mean?'" He says that frequently they respond,

*S*ome teens become vegetarians because they do not like meat. However, if they do not like vegetables either, they may put their health at risk from eating a poor diet.

"'It means I'm not going to eat any more meat, eggs or dairy products.' 'OK, what *will* you eat?' I ask. Too often the answer is, 'Chips, bread, whole wheat cookies.'"[2]

That, Leach points out, is not a balanced diet. "When I ask about vegetables like lima beans and spinach, the answer too often is, 'I'm not crazy about those.' But the truth is, you cannot be a vegetarian without vegetables. Too many kids say they are not 'into' meat, but they also are not 'into' vegetables."[3]

Several things in the teenage lifestyle make it hard for teens to get everything they need in a vegetarian diet, Dr. Leach says. One is lack of information and not doing careful meal planning. "That is not a knock on teens," he explains. "They have an active lifestyle and not much time." Also, he adds, vegetarian meals are not easy to get in many school cafeterias and fast-food places.[4]

# Getting Enough Calories and Fat

Teenagers who eat a vegetarian diet that is not carefully planned to include all the nutrients the body needs can run into many different problems. First of all, Dr. Leach says, a vegetarian teen may have a hard time taking in enough calories. "Vegetarian foods have a higher volume and a lower calorie count than nonvegetarian foods," he says. "They are not heavy in fat, which is a source of calories. You have to eat a lot on a vegetarian diet, you have to be full all the time to get enough calories. I find a lot of kids on this diet lose weight, thin down, do not fill out the way kids on nonvegetarian diets do."

Fat, he points out, is not all bad, even though many people think they should not eat any. "Fat provides some things you need," Dr. Leach says. "The body uses it to make hormones and to coat nerves."[5] But, he says, by keeping fat intake around 30 percent of your diet and by looking for unsaturated rather than saturated fat, you can stay healthy.

Check food labels to find out what kind of fat the food contains. There are not as many sources of fat in vegetarian diets, but nuts, seeds and peanut butter have it. Snacks such as dried fruit or crackers with cheese or peanut butter can add calories to help avoid unwanted weight loss.

*N*uts are high in both calories and nutrients, including protein and fat. They can be an important part of a vegetarian diet.

# Getting the Right Vitamins and Minerals

Not eating dairy products could cause a calcium deficiency. Bones are constantly repairing and rebuilding themselves throughout life; calcium is the building material. An old woman in a wheelchair because of a broken hip may have had weak, brittle bones from lack of calcium. So why worry about what might happen fifty or more years from now? Because strong bones are built during the teen years. "Now is the time when you really want to thicken your bones, get them sturdy, build up your lifetime strength," says Dr. Leach.[6] Calcium is also needed for other things such as energy and strength.

Although some calcium is found in dark green vegetables, it would be hard to eat enough of them to get all the calcium bones need. Vegetarians who do not drink milk or eat other dairy products need to find another source. Soy milk can help, but it does not have as much calcium as cow's milk. Some orange juice has added calcium, so it can be a good choice. Calcium supplements, found in any drugstore, may be needed. They come in different forms, such as tablets to swallow or chew and with or without added vitamin D. Some antacid products also have a lot of calcium.

Dr. Leach points out that certain foods may stop the body from taking in calcium. Phosphate in soda can cause the kidneys to flush out calcium, and the acids in some vegetables, such as spinach, can make the body absorb less calcium.[7]

A person following a vegan diet does not eat any animal products, including eggs and dairy products. This can put the person at risk for not getting enough vitamin B-12, which is found only in animal products. It is needed to make healthy red blood cells. Not getting enough can cause anemia (a blood condition), bleeding into muscles and joints, spongy gums, and slow wound healing.[8] Some cereals have it, but many do not. Read labels to be sure. Vegans who are not getting vitamin B-12 from a cereal may need to take it in a vitamin tablet; check with a doctor first.

Not getting enough iron is a risk on a vegetarian diet. Lack of iron causes anemia, pale skin, tiredness, and weakness.[9] Dried fruits and grains are a good source of iron—raisins on cereal do more than

*D*ark green vegetables contain some calcium. However, it would be nearly impossible to eat enough of them to reach the body's daily requirement. Vegetarians who do not eat dairy products usually need to find another source of calcium to supplement their diet.

make it taste good. Most breads and cereals have added iron. Some soy milk does also. Again, check the label.

Vegetarian diets can also be low in zinc. Lack of this mineral can cause fatigue, inability to taste or smell well, abnormal growth, and slow healing of cuts and scrapes.[10] Zinc comes from nuts, peanut butter, beans, peas, whole grains, cereals with added minerals, and soy milk. A high fiber diet (which most vegetarian diets are) can make the body absorb zinc poorly.[11]

# What About Protein?

Many vegetarians worry about not getting enough protein, which the body uses to build muscles, blood, skin, hair, nails, and the internal organs. Not having enough protein causes slow growth in children, weakness, muscle wasting, depression, and an inability to fight infections.[12] Most Americans eat more protein than they need. However, says Dr. Wang-Cheng of the Medical College of Wisconsin, a diet of only fruit and green vegetables could lead to protein deficiency.

Vegetarians used to be warned that plant proteins are not complete like animal proteins are. They do not have all the amino acids, or "building blocks," the body needs. To get complete proteins they were told to eat plant products together in certain combinations—beans and rice, for example. "That's now become less important," she says. "Research shows if you eat a balanced diet each day that includes nuts, grains, and legumes (beans) you will get enough protein."[13] The proteins do not have to be complete at each meal, she says, as long as they balance out in the total diet. But without

# Guide to Legumes

*"Legumes" is another name for peas and beans. They can be used in soups or salads, combined with rice, mixed into tacos or burritos, mashed into a chip dip, or spread on sandwiches. Here are several different kinds of legumes that can be used in a vegetarian diet.*

**black beans**—dark colored beans. Used in Mexican foods such as tacos or burritos, or served as a side dish.

**black-eyed peas**—greenish-tan peas with a black dot. Cooked as a side dish, served over rice, and used in soups and stews.

**garbanzo beans (chickpeas)**—large yellow or white-gray beans; often found on salad bars. Mashed, they are used in hummus, a spread for dips or sandwiches. They can be seasoned with lemon, olive oil, or garlic. Often used in three bean salads.

**kidney beans**—red beans. Used in chili and three-bean salads.

**lentils**—small, smooth, gray-green beans. Often used in lentil soup, stews, and casseroles.

**soy beans**—small, whitish beans. Used in the same ways as lentils.

**pinto beans**—tan and white beans. Often used for refried beans and other Mexican foods.

**split peas**—bright green or yellow dry peas. Often used in soup.

**white beans ("navy" or "northern" beans)**—small white beans. Used in thick soups, stews, and casseroles.

legumes or a soy protein source, it can be hard to get enough protein.

# Other Potential Problems

Not a health problem, but a possible social problem, is the fact that the body sometimes makes a lot of intestinal gas at the beginning of a vegetarian diet. The body has to get used to the extra fiber. The problem can last several weeks. It can be made less severe by changing to a vegetarian diet slowly rather than all at once. Steaming vegetables instead of eating them raw can also help by breaking down the fiber. Digestive enzyme products to relieve gas problems are sold in drugstores.

Vegetarians are not as likely to have harmful bacteria such as salmonella or E. coli in their food as

## Some Warning Signs of an Eating Disorder

*A vegetarian diet can help with weight control. But if a teen carries it too far, it can be dangerous. Any of the following may be a sign of trouble:*

✓family and friends say the teen is getting too thin

✓his or her hair becomes thin and dry

✓he or she constantly feels cold

✓her menstrual periods stop

*Teens should consult with a doctor or dietitian for advice on how to control weight but still eat healthily.*[14]

meat eaters are. But germs can live on many fruits and vegetables. People have gotten E. coli infections from raspberries, unpasteurized apple juice, and alfalfa sprouts. Some have gotten hepatitis (a viral disease of the liver) from strawberries. Some have even died from these infections. "Wash everything very well, especially sprouts," Dr. Wang-Cheng warns. "They are moist so germs can grow in them."[15]

Some doctors and mental health professionals have warned that, in some cases, becoming a vegetarian may be a warning sign of an eating disorder such as anorexia nervosa, in which a person fears weight gain and stops eating. According to the American Anorexia/Bulimia Association, over 90 percent of anorexia patients are girls or women. It is most common between the ages of twelve and seventeen.[16] About one percent of teenage girls in the United States become anorexic. Nearly ten percent of them may die from not eating.[17] A psychology professor, Dr. Ruth Striegel-Moore, says being a vegetarian can be a hidden way of dieting, a way to cut out fat.[18]

"Some [people with eating disorders] are truly vegetarian and have been for a long time, but for some, it's just another way of rationalizing their diets," says Ron Thompson, Ph.D. Thompson is co-director of an eating disorders program and author of a book about athletes and eating disorders. He says the number of his patients who say they are vegetarian has increased from about one quarter to a third. David Herzog, M.D., director of the Harvard Eating Disorder Center at Massachusetts General Hospital, also finds about a third of his patients are vegetarians. Sheri Weitz, R.D., a nutrition therapist at the Radar Institute's eating disorder center, says that there it is almost half.[19]

Anne Sprenger, R.D., is a dietitian who specializes in working with clients with eating disorders. "Nine out of ten of my clients, when I first talk to them, tell me they are vegetarians," she says. "I think being a vegetarian can be a way to drop a whole food group. The real reason these teens become vegetarian is not to get healthier, but to cut fats and calories and to lose weight. They may say, 'I don't eat anything that had a face', but that's not what it's really about for them."[20] An eating disorder, Sprenger says, can result in low energy, poor growth in teens who have not finished growing, poor hair and skin quality, low muscle mass development in boys, and a menstrual cycle that becomes irregular or stops for girls.[21]

Both Dr. Leach and Dr. Wang-Cheng offer one last warning: Teen vegetarians should not use vegetarianism as an excuse to live on junk food. "Just not eating meat doesn't mean you will have a good diet," Dr. Wang-Cheng says. "You can get plenty of junk food that is heavy on sugar, salt, and fat in a vegetarian diet. Vegetarians can eat a lot of empty calories [calories with no nutrition] even if they are vegetarian calories!"[22]

"The kids I see who do best on a vegetarian diet are those who are lacto-ovo vegetarians," says Dr. Leach. "It is much harder on a vegan diet. I think kids who want to do this should be sure they aren't doing it just because it's the fashionable thing, but is a real nutritional decision they are making. Then they need to learn a lot about nutrition and plan their meals carefully."[23]

# Chapter 5

# Planning a Healthy Diet

**C**an a vegetarian get everything needed for good health without eating meat? The answer is yes, but only if the person takes the time to learn what the body needs and how to get it from a meatless diet. Just trying to live on apples, carrots, and rice will not work. That diet is unhealthy.

## The Digestive System

Human beings need to eat certain types and amounts of food to stay healthy. The human body has a digestive system to process food and get rid of waste. It can be thought of as a long, twisting tube made up of a series of organs. The organs that make up the digestive system, sometimes called the digestive tract, are the mouth, throat, esophagus, stomach, small intestine, large intestine, rectum, and anus. The digestive system also includes some organs that are not directly attached. These are the pancreas, liver, and gall bladder.[1]

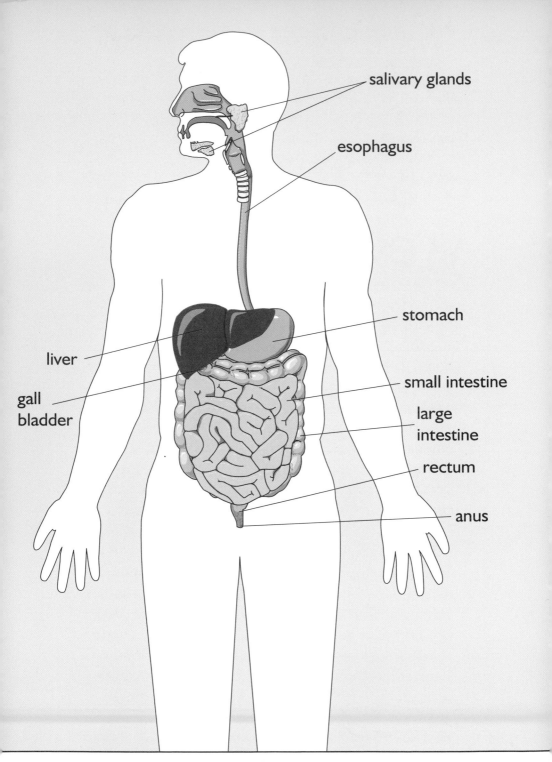

salivary glands

esophagus

stomach

liver

small intestine

gall
bladder

large
intestine

rectum

anus

*T*he digestive system processes food for energy and eliminates waste.

Food starts its trip through the digestive tract when it enters the mouth. There, teeth and saliva begin to break down the food. Swallowing moves the chewed food into the esophagus. The organs in the digestive system contract in rhythmic waves to move the food along. That is called peristalsis. The food enters the stomach, where chemicals called enzymes break the food down and take the nutrients from it. That process is called digestion. Then the food goes into the small intestine, where more digestion takes place.

The small intestine is especially important. This is where the nutrients are absorbed into the bloodstream so they can go where they are needed in the body. The food mass left over after digestion is waste. It moves into the large intestine, which absorbs most of the water from it. Once the waste is solid, it travels to the colon. It is stored there until it passes from the body through the rectum and anus during a bowel movement.[2]

This system is delicately balanced. Many things can throw it off. Poor diet, stress, and sicknesses caused by bacteria or viruses can all upset the digestive system. This can result in conditions such as constipation, when waste is not eliminated, or diarrhea, when the waste becomes too liquid. Eating a well balanced diet is one thing that can help keep the digestive system healthy.

Medical researchers think that fiber is important to a healthy diet. Fiber is the part of plant food our bodies cannot digest. As it passes through the digestive system, fiber acts like a sponge absorbing water. That keeps the waste soft and traveling quickly through the system. People who eat enough fiber are less likely to be constipated or have other bowel

# Two Diets to Avoid

**The Macrobiotic Diet**—This diet originally came from Japan. It doesn't allow the person to eat much—mostly brown rice and certain vegetables. According to dietitian Anne Sprenger, it is a dangerous diet. "It is supposed to cleanse the body," she says, "but the danger is that people on this diet can die. There isn't enough in the diet to allow life and growth, especially for a young, growing person. A person on this diet slowly starves to death."

She points out that even if a person ate enough brown rice and vegetables to provide the calories he or she needed (and that would take a lot), there still would not be enough protein to stay healthy. The person's muscles would slowly waste away.[3]

**A Fruitarian Diet**—Some people go so far as to drop even vegetables from their diet, eating only fruits. A fruitarian diet may include squash, tomatoes, seeds, and nuts. Some also eat vegetable oils and honey. This is not a balanced diet and does not include enough protein, according to Sprenger. It has the same dangers as the macrobiotic diet.[4]

problems. Some scientists think that fiber may help protect against colon cancer and heart disease.[5]

Fiber is found in fruits, vegetables, dried beans and other legumes, grains, and nuts. So a balanced vegetarian diet is high in fiber.

# A Healthy Diet

There are many sources of information on how to plan a healthy vegetarian diet. The first stop might be a bookstore or the library. There are many books on vegetarian eating, and cookbooks with vegetarian recipes fill the shelves. Pick up a few and read them before beginning to plan meals.

There is also a lot of information on healthy vegetarian eating on the Internet. Many vegetarian groups have Web sites. Some of them are just for teenagers. Some contain general information on vegetarian eating. Others have recipes and tips for vegetarian cooking. Using any search engine and typing in the key word "vegetarian" will turn up a huge list of sites. Visit different sites to find the most useful ones.

Dietitians can help with planning a healthy vegetarian diet. They can be found in most cities. Try the local hospital. They all have dietitians on staff and may offer diet planning services. Some dietitians are not part of a hospital staff but are in private practice. They are listed in the Yellow Pages of the telephone book.

A "field trip" to a big supermarket may be useful. Many people are surprised when they see the many meatless foods and meat substitutes at an ordinary food store. Health food stores may offer even more choices in vegetarian foods. Wherever you shop for food, though, be sure to check the food labels for

# Finding Hidden Animal Products

*Some ingredients on food labels may not sound like meat or egg products, but they are. People who wish to avoid eating animal products should check food labels to be sure these ingredients are not included.*

**albumin**—made from egg whites. Used for thickening frosting, pudding, and jellied foods.

**anchovies**—small fish. Used especially in Asian sauces, and sometimes put in salads or on pizza.

**animal shortening**—lard, or pure animal fat. Used in baked goods and refried beans. Look instead for products that use vegetable shortening.

**carmine cochineal**—red food coloring made from an insect. This ingredient is not the same as red vegetable dye.

**casein**—a protein that comes from milk. Sometimes added to soy cheese or milk. The label might say "caseinate."

**lactose**—a milk sugar. Used in many prepared or boxed food products.

**gelatin**—a product from animal bones. Used to thicken foods such as non-fat yogurt, baked goods, and jellied products. Kosher gelatin is vegetarian.

**natural flavorings**—many are from fruits, vegetables, and spices, but some could be from meat or other animal products.

**rennet**—an enzyme from calves. Used in many cheeses. Sometimes the label will only say "enzymes." Some products may specify that they are made with only vegetable enzymes.

**whey**—milk-based. Used in baked goods.

ingredients as well as for nutritional content. Many foods include "hidden" animal products that vegetarians might prefer to avoid.

One way to plan vegetarian meals is to use the vegetarian pyramid, says dietitian Anne Sprenger. "Obviously, this pyramid is different from the regular food pyramid because there is no meat group," she says. "Milk and milk substitutes, and meat/fish/poultry substitutes such as soy and tofu, replace the meat group. The number of servings of fruit, vegetables and grains is also higher."[6]

Here are the basics the body needs, and ways to get them from a vegetarian diet.

*Protein.* This is what people worry about most in a vegetarian diet. It is an important concern, but it

*S*oy products such as tofu, soy milk, and soy burgers can be an important part of a vegetarian diet. Many mainstream food markets now carry such items.

# Vegetarian Food Guide Pyramid[7]

Fats, Oils, & Sweets
Use sparingly

Milk, Yogurt, &
Cheese Group
0–3
servings
daily*

Dry Beans, Nuts,
Seeds, Eggs, and
Meat Substitutes Group
2–3
servings
daily

Vegetable
Group
3–5
servings
daily

Fruit
Group
2–4
servings
daily

Bread, Cereal, Rice, & Pasta Group
6–11 servings daily

*Vegetarians who choose not to use milk, yogurt, or cheese need to select other food sources that are rich in calcium.

may not be as much of an issue as people think. Many Americans eat too much protein, more than the body needs, in a meat-based diet. Vegetarians can go too far in the opposite direction and not get enough. "The body needs six to seven ounces of protein a day," says Sprenger. "A cup of beans has one ounce, a veggie burger, about two ounces, compared to a hamburger's four."[8] So a vegetarian may need to eat more food to get the same amount of protein.

The vegetarian food pyramid suggests two to three servings from the dry beans, nuts, seeds, eggs, and meat substitutes group a day. A serving might be a cup of soy milk, a half cup of cooked beans or peas, one egg or two egg whites, two tablespoons of nuts or seeds, a quarter cup of tofu, or two tablespoons of peanut butter. Nonmeat protein can also come from cheese, milk, yogurt, or texturized vegetable protein. Remember, it is not necessary to combine grains to get complete proteins in each meal. Experts now say that eating a variety of sources throughout the day will do the job.[9]

Lacto-ovo vegetarians, who eat dairy products and eggs, usually do not have a protein problem if they eat a wide variety of vegetables, grains, egg dishes, and dairy products. But they should think about how much fat they are getting in the dairy products and eggs. One study of vegetarians found that some of them eat almost as much fat as meat-eaters.[10] Low-fat milk and cheese can help, as can eating only the whites of eggs.

Vegans, who do not eat any animal products, have a harder time getting enough protein. Soy products, dried beans and other legumes, and nuts can provide enough protein. Vegans must be sure, however, to eat a big enough variety of those foods in large enough portions to meet their body's protein needs.

*Carbohydrates.* Vegetarians get their carbohydrates, the body's main source of energy, the same way nonvegetarians do, from grains. "Just don't get them all from sugars," Sprenger warns. "Have a nice balance of breads, cereals, and pasta."[11] That will also help give the body the fiber it needs for good digestive health.

*Calcium.* For lacto-ovo vegetarians, getting enough calcium is easy. For vegans, it is a lot harder. Experts say that the teen years are the most important for building strong bones. This cannot be done without calcium. Vegans can get some calcium from tofu, sesame butter, and green leafy vegetables such as collard greens, mustard greens, and kale. If someone does not like tofu or those vegetables, another source might be orange juice with added calcium. "Many vegans will probably need a supplement," Sprenger says.[12] It is best to check with a doctor before taking any supplements.

*Iron.* Teens need a lot of iron. Foods with large amounts of iron include broccoli, raisins, spinach, black-eyed peas, chickpeas, and pinto beans. To help the body absorb the iron, eat a food that has vitamin C, such as a citrus fruit or juice, tomatoes, or berries, at the same meal.

*Vitamin B-12.* Because it comes only from animal products, some vegetarians have a hard time getting enough vitamin B-12 by diet alone. This is especially true for vegans. They will usually need a supplement (again, check with a doctor before taking any supplements). Some cereals have added iron and vitamin B-12. Read the label to be sure.

*Calories.* It can be hard to get enough calories on a vegetarian diet, because many vegetarian foods are low in fat and calories. This is especially true for physically active teens. In general, teenage girls need about 2,200 calories a day, and teenage boys need about 2,800.[13] If a person loses too much weight on a vegetarian diet, one solution is to add more calorie-dense foods such as dairy products and nut butters. They are healthier than high-sugar foods such as baked goods.

*E*ating certain foods in combination can help the body absorb the nutrients in those foods. Citrus fruits are high in vitamin C, which helps the body absorb iron from iron-rich foods.

Some foods can make a vegetarian's life easier because they are so much like meat in flavor and texture that they can easily take its place. For example, some people call eggplant the "vegetarian's beef" because it has a meaty texture. Chop it and add with mushrooms to pasta sauces, casseroles, and soups. It can also be sliced, steamed, and covered with pasta sauce and melted cheese.

Tofu can be used in stir-fries, sauces, and soups in place of meat. Tofu alone has almost no taste, but it will take on the flavor of the foods mixed with it. Tofu is a meat substitute that many vegetarians enjoy experimenting with in recipes. They try it in many creative ways: mixed into chip dips, crumbled over other foods, stirred into egg dishes, and sliced and sprinkled with spices in sandwiches. Bulgur wheat can be used in similar ways.

Chopped, cooked beans can be used in place of hamburger in pasta sauce and tacos. Beans can be used in many dishes, from red beans and rice to chili, cold rice, and bean salads. They can be mashed to use in dips or spread on sandwiches. Some people like to munch on them cold, flavored with spices, as snacks. Precooked canned beans are easier to use than dry beans, because dry beans usually need to be soaked in water overnight before cooking.

Almond, cashew, sesame, and soy butters can be a nice change from peanut butter as a source of protein. They are good spread on whole grain toast or bagels at breakfast, on crackers for a snack, or in lunchtime sandwiches. Keep in mind that they are high in fat.

Dietitian Anne Sprenger suggests that teens thinking about becoming vegetarians try some vegetarian dishes first before deciding. What you do not like, you probably will not eat! "Kids, especially in their early teens, may not realize what kinds of things they need to eat to be a vegetarian," Sprenger says. "Many of them don't think beans are great unless they are in a bean dip! They many not like tofu, red beans and rice, or lentil soup. Go to a vegetarian deli or Indian or Asian restaurant and try some foods to see if you can eat them. Then get a vegetarian cookbook and try some of the dishes to see if you like them."[14]

Teens thinking about becoming vegetarians should also ask themselves if they are open-minded enough to be willing to try different foods and learn to like them. People who do not like foods that are different from what they are used to will probably not be very happy vegetarians.

Sprenger reminds teens that being a successful vegetarian takes work. It takes learning, planning, and some special cooking skills. "If you do this, you have to do it right," she says. "If you don't eat right or if you eat only a few foods, especially if they are high in fat and low in nutrition, you won't be the best you can be. It will affect how you perform in school and on the athletic field. It will affect your mood. Being a vegetarian can be fine if the person is willing to learn and really likes vegetarian foods. But kids have to think carefully about whether this is a good choice for them."[15]

# "So, You Want to Be a Vegetarian . . . "

Teens who want to become vegetarians may find it difficult to break the news to their parents and others. Some people may support the decision, while others may disapprove. And some people may not know a lot about vegetarianism themselves.

Lots of parents worry when their kids become vegetarians. Here are a few things teens can do to make it easier on their parents.

- Pick a good time to talk about your decision. Making an announcement when there is family tension about something else, or right in the middle of a holiday dinner, may not be the best approach.

- Stay calm. Parents will be much more open to listening if you discuss the issue in a reasonable way. On the other hand, saying things like "I'm doing this, and you can't stop me!" will probably result in everyone becoming upset and angry.

- Explain that you will take the time to learn about being a healthy vegetarian, and will share what you learn with your parents. Going to a dietitian first is also a good idea.

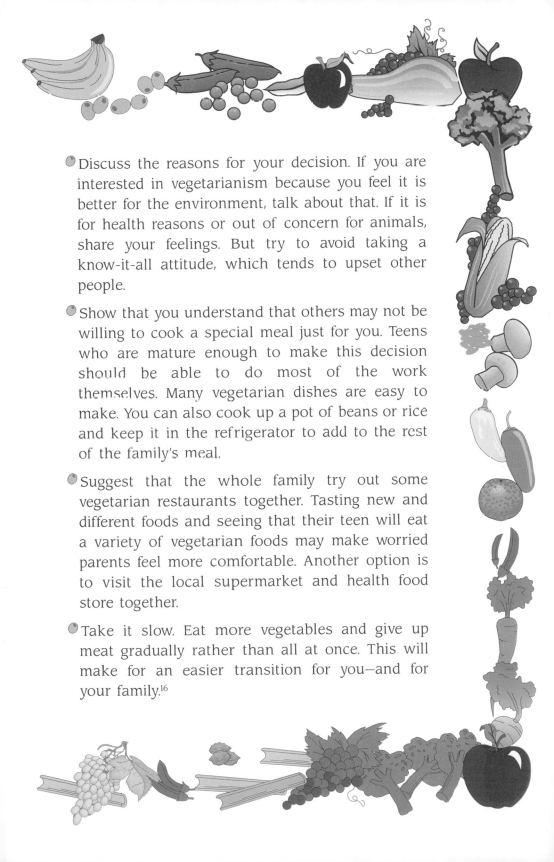

● Discuss the reasons for your decision. If you are interested in vegetarianism because you feel it is better for the environment, talk about that. If it is for health reasons or out of concern for animals, share your feelings. But try to avoid taking a know-it-all attitude, which tends to upset other people.

● Show that you understand that others may not be willing to cook a special meal just for you. Teens who are mature enough to make this decision should be able to do most of the work themselves. Many vegetarian dishes are easy to make. You can also cook up a pot of beans or rice and keep it in the refrigerator to add to the rest of the family's meal.

● Suggest that the whole family try out some vegetarian restaurants together. Tasting new and different foods and seeing that their teen will eat a variety of vegetarian foods may make worried parents feel more comfortable. Another option is to visit the local supermarket and health food store together.

● Take it slow. Eat more vegetables and give up meat gradually rather than all at once. This will make for an easier transition for you—and for your family.[16]

## Organizations

**Vegetarian Resource Group (VRG)**
P.O. Box 1463
Baltimore, MD 21203
(410) 366-8343

**Vegan Action**
P.O. Box 4353
Berkeley, CA 94704-6297
(510) 548-7377

**North American Vegetarian Society**
P.O. Box 72
Dolgeville, NY 13329
(518) 568-7970

**Vegetarian Youth Network**
P.O. Box 1141
New Paltz, NY 12561

## Internet Addresses

**Vegetarian Resource Group (VRG)**
<http://www.vrg.org>

**Vegan Action**
<http://www.vegan.org>

**North American Vegetarian Society**
<http://www.navs-online.org>

## Chapter 1. Meet Some Vegetarians

1. Personal interview with Lynn Isherwood, December 17, 1998.

2. Ibid.

3. Ibid.

4. Ibid.

5. Ibid.

6. Ibid.

7. Ibid.

8. Ibid.

9. Ibid.

10. Kristie Hertz, "Life as a Teenage Vegetarian," *The Vegetarian Journal*, January/February 1995, <http://www.veg.on.ca/newsletr/julaug95/teenage.html> (May 10, 1999).

11. Personal interview with Brad Winkler, January 22, 2000.

12. Judy Krizmanic, "Prisoners of the Plate," *Vegetarian Times*, April, 1995, p. 104.

## Chapter 2. Who Is a Vegetarian?

1. Adapted from "Vegetarianism, Is It OK for Children?" *MayoClinic Healthoasis*, July 6, 1998, and "Vegging Out," *Teen*, February, 1995.

2. "Vegetarianism in a Nutshell," Vegetarian Resource Group, August 30, 2000, <http://www.vrg.org/nutshell/poll2000.htm> (November 3, 2000).

3. American Medical Association, *Reader's Guide to Alternative Health Methods* (Milwaukee, Wisc.: American Medical Association, 1993), pp. 258–259.

4. "Famous Vegetarians," n.d., <http://www.famousveggie.com/peoplenew.cfm> (November 2, 2000).

5. Ibid.

## Chapter 3. Why Become a Vegetarian?

1. "Paleolithic Diet vs. Vegetarianism," *Beyond Vegetarianism*, 1998 <http://www.beyondveg.com> (April 15, 2000).

2. "The Truth Hurts," Farm Sanctuary, April 13, 2000 <http://www.factoryfarming.com> (April 15, 2000).

3. Alan Durning and Holly Brough, "Taking Stock: Animal Farming and the Environment," Worldwatch Institute, Washington, D.C., July 1991; quoted in Judy Krizmanic, *A Teen's Guide to Going Vegetarian* (New York: Puffin Books, 1994), p. 25.

4. Earthsave Foundation, "Our Food, Our World: The Realities of an Animal-Based Diet," *Earthsave*, Santa Cruz, 1992; quoted in Krizmanic, p. 27.

5. Nancy Ryan, "Animal Rights Is Prime Motivator for Teen Vegetarians," *Chicago Tribune*, August 7, 1995.

6. Center for Science in the Public Interest, "Safe Food: Eating Wisely in a Risky World," (Los Angeles, Calif.: Living Planet, 1991); quoted in Krizmanic, p. 59.

7. Tom Kertscher, "E. coli Linked to Sizzler Hygiene," *The Milwaukee Journal Sentinel*, October 31, 2000, pp. 1A, 8A.

8. Telephone interview with Rebekah Wang-Cheng, M.D., January 26, 1999.

9. Telephone interview with Joan Pleuss, R.D., January 20, 1999.

10. *New England Journal of Medicine*, August 3, 1995; quoted in "Vegetarianism: Is It OK for Children?" *MayoClinic Healthoasis*, July 6, 1998.

11. L.J. Beilin, "Vegetarian and Other Complex Diets, Fats, Fibers, and Hypertension," *American Journal of Clinical Nutrition*, Supplement 59, 1988, pp. 712–738.

12. "Vegetarianism: Is It OK for Children?" *MayoClinic Healthoasis*, July 6, 1998.

13. Telephone interview with Pleuss, R.D.

## Chapter 4. Precautions to Keep in Mind

1. Telephone interview with Craig Leach, D.O., January 25, 2000.

2. Ibid.

3. Ibid.

4. Ibid.

5. Ibid.

6. Ibid.

7. Ibid.

8. Thomas Manning, *Mosby's Medical and Nursing Dictionary* (St. Louis: Mosby Company, 1983), p. 1142.

9. Ibid, p. 582.

10. Ibid, p. 1162.

11. Delia Hannock, "You Know I Don't Eat Meat!," *Good Housekeeping*, April 1996, p. 110.

12. Manning, p. 897.

13. Telephone interview with Rebekah Wang-Cheng, M.D., January 26, 1999.

14. Telephone interview with Anne Sprenger, R.D., April 14, 1999.

15. Telephone interview with Wang-Cheng, M.D.

16. Linda Smith, "Teens: Going Green & Lean . . . But Some Are Going Too Far," EGW Publications, 1998, <http://www.naturalland.com/nv/nkds/vegteen.htm> (May 10, 1999).

17. Ibid.

18. Ruth Striegel-Moore, quoted in "Children of the Corn," *Newsweek*, August 28, 1995, pp. 60–62.

19. Judy Krizmanic, "Prisoners of the Plate," *Vegetarian Times*, April, 1995, pp. 101–102.

20. Telephone interview with Sprenger, R.D.

21. Ibid.

22. Telephone interview with Wang-Cheng, M.D.

23. Telephone interview with Leach, D.O.

## Chapter 5. Planning a Healthy Diet

1. Simeon Margolis, ed., *The Johns Hopkins Medical Handbook* (New York: Rebus, Inc., 1992), pp. 170–171.

2. Robert Berkow, Mark H. Beers, eds., *The Merck Manual of Medical Information* (Whitehouse Station, N.J.: Merck & Company, Inc., 1999), pp. 480–484.

3. Telephone interview with Anne Sprenger, R.D., April 14, 1999.

4. Ibid.

5. Theresa Lane, ed., *Foods That Harm, Foods That Heal* (Pleasantville, N.Y.: The Reader's Digest Association, 1998), pp. 145–146.

6. Telephone interview with Sprenger, R.D.

7. National Center for Nutrition and Dietetics. The American Dietetic Association; Based on the USDA Food Guide Pyramid. © ADAF 1997.

8. Telephone interview with Sprenger, R.D.

9. Reed Mangels, Ph.D., R.D., "Vegetarian Nutrition for Teenagers," 1999, <http://www.vegsource.com/nutrition/teennutrition.htm> (November 13, 2000). Reprinted from the Vegetarian Resource Group, Baltimore, Md.

10. Mary Hubbard, Ph.D., R.D., "Scaling the Vegetarian Pyramid," *Better Homes and Gardens*, June, 1994, p. 98.

11. Telephone interview with Sprenger, R.D.

12. Ibid.

13. Charles Clayman, M.D., *The American Medical Association Family Medical Guide*, 3rd ed. (New York: Random House, 1994), p. 29.

14. Telephone interview with Sprenger, R.D.

15. Ibid.

16. Adapted from Judy Krizmanic, *A Teen's Guide to Going Vegetarian* (New York: Puffin Books, 1994), pp. 77–78; personal interview with Lynn Isherwood, December 17, 1998; and telephone interview with Joan Pleuss, R.D., January 20, 1999.

**calcium**—A mineral the body needs to build strong bones and teeth. Calcium is found in dairy products, some dark green vegetables, sardines, and canned salmon.

**carbohydrates**—The nutrients that the body burns as energy fuel. Found in grains and vegetables, carbohydrates are a necessary part of a healthy diet.

**cholesterol**—A fat that comes only from animal products. Too much cholesterol can lead to clogged arteries and heart attacks.

**dietitian**—A person with training in human nutrition who helps clients plan their diets. Registered dietitians may use the initials R. D. (registered dietitian) after their names.

**ethnic food**—Food eaten by people from a certain country or culture. Many ethnic foods are vegetarian, especially those from India, China, and other Asian countries.

**fat**—A nutrient the body uses for energy and to build cells, make hormones, and cushion body organs. Most doctors say no more than thirty percent of a person's diet should come from fat.

**fiber**—A part of some foods that the body cannot digest. The body needs fiber to help it get rid of waste. Fiber also reduces the level of cholesterol in the blood.

**grains**—Seeds from plants such as corn and wheat that are ground into flour and used in baked goods and cereals.

**iron**—A mineral the body needs for blood to carry oxygen to all the organs.

**legumes**—Another name for peas and beans, a common source of protein in vegetarian diets.

**protein**—A nutrient the body uses to build and repair tissues for normal growth.

**soy milk**—A milk-like drink made from soybeans. It usually includes added nutrients that vegetarians need.

**texturized vegetable protein**—A meat substitute made from soybeans. It comes in flakes, or in small pieces that look like browned hamburger meat. It can be pressed into patties like hamburgers or into tubes like hot dogs.

**tofu**—A food made from soybeans. It is white and usually has a sponge-like texture. Tofu does not have much flavor by itself, but it takes on the flavor of accompanying ingredients and seasonings.

**whole wheat flour**—Whole wheat flour, unlike white flour, is made from whole kernels of wheat. It is an important part of a vegetarian diet because of all the vitamins and minerals it contains.

Anderson, Jean, and Barbara Deskins. *The Nutrition Bible: a Comprehensive No-Nonsense Reference Guide to Foods, Nutrients, Additives, Preservatives, Pollutants, and Everything Else We Eat and Drink*. New York: Morrow, 1995.

Krizmanic, Judy. *A Teen's Guide to Going Vegetarian*. New York: Puffin Books, 1994.

Krizmanic, Judy. *A Teen's Guide to Vegetarian Cooking*. New York: Viking Penguin, 1999.

Messina, Virginia and Mark. *The Vegetarian Way: Healthy Eating for You and Your Family*. New York: Crown Publishers, 1996.

Nardo, Don. *Vitamins and Minerals: The Encyclopedia of Health*. New York: Chelsea House, 1994.

Pierson, Stephanie. *Vegetables Rock! A Complete Guide for Teenage Vegetarians*. New York: Bantam, Doubleday, Dell Publishing, 1999.

Salter, Charles. *The Vegetarian Teen*. Brookfield, Conn.: Millbrook Press, 1991.

Serafin, Kim. *Everything You Need to Know about Being a Vegetarian*. New York: The Rosen Publishing Group, Inc., 1999.

Weiss, Stephanie I. *Everything You Need to Know about Being a Vegan*. New York: The Rosen Publishing Group, Inc., 1999.

Further Reading